PREPPER'S LONG-TERM
SURVIVAL GUIDE

FOOD | SHELTER | SECURITY | OFF-THE-GRID POWER

AND MORE LIFE-SAVING STRATEGIES FOR MAKING YOUR HOME SELF-RELIANT

NICK REESE

CONTENTS

FORWARD

There are a lot of books out there about survival. The online marketplace, along with digital publishing, has all but eliminated much of the responsibility on the author and publisher. The result has been a glut of poorly written books on survival and other subjects which have been written by people who don't have any idea of the subject they are writing about. The writers are often young professional writers, who merely look up what they can find about a given topic and rewrite it into their own words.

A large part of the problem with this system is that the people writing these books don't have enough knowledge to judge the veracity of the information they are finding in their internet research; don't know how to prioritize it and don't know how to make sure that the books they write will truly help people solve their problems. Sadly, neither do many of the publishers.

So, what's different about this book?

To put it in a word… me. When you buy this book, you're buying 47 years of survival experience. I got my start as a survivalist while I was in high school, during the latter years of the Cold War. Like many of my generation, we lived in fear that Moscow and Washington would lose it one day and "push the button, " destroying both our countries in thermonuclear war.

But unlike many of my peers, I let my fear drive me to action. At the time, I lived near the Rocky Mountains and I discovered that I could get to the back side of that first mountain in 20 minutes. Since we were supposed to get 30 minutes warning, once the button was pushed, that gave me a chance at survival. So, I started studying, learning everything I could on how to survive.

Now, 47 years later, I'm still learning. Studying survival is a normal part of my routine. I build my own survival equipment, have my own survival garden and train in survival skills. Everything in this book is either something I'm doing or something I've done in the past. It's practical knowledge, coming from someone who lives this life.

That's what you're getting.

INTRODUCTION

As we look at time from this side of 2020, it seems that the outbreak of the COVID-19 pandemic was a dividing line between past and present. On the other side of the line, things were fairly good, with occasional problems that we all dealt with. But once we crossed into 2020, problems became nonstop. These weren't just any problems either; they were disasters, which followed one after another. It seemed like each month had its own disaster, to the point where people were making jokes about "disaster pools" and asking who had guessed the right disaster for that month.

The trend continued through 2020, 2021 and into 2022. At this point, nobody really knows how long it is going to continue. This could be the "new normal," totally replacing the normal that we all knew and loved. Granted, that normal had problems too; but not to the scale that this new normal does.

Actually, this is not the first time in recent history when we have been faced with years that seemed to be filled with disasters. The year of Hurricane Katrina, 2005, was one such year. People were talking about the world ending at that time; but the world managed to keep spinning on. Likewise, there have been years where we were facing potential disasters that seemed as bad. Does anyone remember Y2K? Yet that wasn't even a fizzle, let alone a bang.

If we look back through history, there have been plenty of disasters which have struck at one time or another. Sometimes they strike singly and in other years it seems that they come all together in a bunch. 2020 and the years to follow, have definitely been years which were filled with many problems.

When the COVID-19 pandemic was first announced, it didn't seem like a big deal. That was something happening on the other side of the world and probably wouldn't affect us. But that attitude didn't last long, when the first COVID-19 patient died in the United States, a mere 10 days after we first heard about it and the various state governments started declaring lockdowns three months later. About the same time, supermarkets started emptying out; first of hand sanitizer, then toilet paper and then just about everything else. We went from full grocery stores to empty ones in one week, and the supply problems still haven't gotten back to normal, over two years later.

Yet there were people in our society who weren't in as bad a shape as the rest of the population. These people had stockpiles of toilet paper and other supplies in their homes; not because they beat everyone else to the grocery store, but because they lived that way.

These "preppers" believed in being prepared for any disaster, stockpiling supplies, buying survival gear and learning the necessary skills to survive in any given disaster.

Although the prepping movement is relatively new, the concept of prepping is not. If we go back in history, we find that throughout the majority of history, our ancestors have been forced to prepare. If nothing else, they would be faced by a disaster called "winter" every year. During that time, they would be unable to hunt, trap, forage or grow food. If they didn't have enough food stocked up, before the first snows of winter came, their chances of survival through the winter were very slim.

It is only in modern times, when we have built a massive infrastructure and incredibly complex supply chain that people have forgotten about the need to prepare for winter and other disasters. We have become less and less self-sufficient, while we have become more and more dependent on that supply chain and infrastructure. As long as everything keeps working, we're fine. But as we've seen in 2020 and 2021, it doesn't take much to make the whole house of cards fall down.

Of the entire infrastructure, the electric grid is the most fragile part. Yet we need electricity for just about everything we do. it's safe to say that one cannot live long, in modern society, without it. People lived without it in the past and there are still parts of the world where people live without it today; but they know how to live without it. We, on the other hand, have little to no idea of how to live without electricity and we don't have the tools to do many common, necessary tasks, without using electricity to power our tools.

But electricity isn't the whole problem. We also need our infrastructure to provide us with water and to carry waste water away from our homes. We need natural gas for cooking and heating. We need countless things that society brings us, from communications to people to protect us from the two-legged predators living in this world.

Then there's the supply chain. A century ago, most products were manufactured locally, if not in one's own town, then in a city not far down the road. While there were merchants which traded goods across vast distances, even across the oceans, those were mostly high-cost luxury goods, not the things we need every day. Today, countless products that we use every day come from the other side of the world. Some start out as raw materials shipped from Africa to Asia, where they are formed into parts, which are shipped to another country for assembly into a finished product. Only then are they shipped here to the United States for sale.

The reality is, we are less capable of surviving a disaster than any other time in history. That's what started the prepping movement and what has caused so many to come on-board. If anything, 2020 and 2021 have proven the preppers rights, given millions of other people good reason to join their ranks. Since you're reading this book; I have to assume you're one of those; or at least considering joining their ranks.

SHORT AND LONG-TERM DISASTERS

Disasters come in all shapes and sizes, from personal disasters that only affect you and your family, to disasters that affect entire countries. In a few rare cases, they affect the whole world. That's actually becoming more common, as the world becomes more interconnected and supply chains become more international, any disaster is likely to have global consequences.

Just take a look at the Russian invasion of Ukraine as an example. Ukraine is the largest country in Europe, yet dwarfed by her neighbor to the east. When Russia attacked, it was necessary for them to draft every able-bodied man, between 18 and 60 years of age. So that attack has affected the entire country.

But that's not all. In response to Russia's invasion, most of the world slapped sanctions on Russia, including trade embargoes. Russia is a major exporter of petroleum products and natural gas. So those trade embargoes managed to raise the cost per barrel of oil considerably. Between the two countries, they produce 35% of the world's wheat. But with the war, neither country is shipping. That is

creating wheat shortages worldwide. On top of that Russia is one of the world's largest producers of potash, which is used in making fertilizers. The impact of countries not being able to buy their potash is yet to be seen, as of this writing.

But not all disasters have a worldwide impact. Some are much more localized, as well as being shorter-term. Hurricane Katrina, Hurricane Sandy and Hurricane Harvey, as bad as they were, were short-term, localized disasters. While a few million people were impacted by each of those hurricanes, those numbers were nothing like the impact of COVID-19.

Hurricanes, like most other natural disasters, are short-term disasters, as the people impacted by them can get back to some semblance of a normal life within a few weeks. Granted, repairing the damage from that disaster may take a few years, especially for those who didn't have adequate insurance coverage. But they don't force the survivors to find a whole new way to live in order to survive.

Long-term disasters are a whole different thing. In the prepping community, they are often referred to as "TEOTWAWKI events," which stands for "The end of the world as we know it." Please note that this doesn't mean the world ends, just that the way we're used to living has to be replaced by something else. Most of the time, it means becoming totally self-sufficient in order to survive, as the aforementioned supply chains and infrastructure are basically gone.

Perhaps the most infamous of these TEOTWAWKI events involve

the loss of the electrical grid. There are several possible scenarios that could cause that to happen, from a massive CME (coronal mass ejection) from the sun, such as the Carrington Event that happened in 1859 (before we had much use for electricity) to an attack by a high-altitude EMP (electromagnetic pulse) from some rogue nation.

Preparing for long-term disasters and short-term disasters aren't the same, although to prepare for a long-term disaster, one must do the things that they would do for short-term disaster preparation, along with some additional preparation. When the disaster struck, they would treat it like a short-term disaster, up until it was clear that it wasn't going to be over in a couple of months. At that time, it would be necessary to begin changing over to a long-term survival strategy.

Actually, there are many preppers who are working on both at the same time, having incorporated some of their long-term strategies into their everyday life. One such strategy is growing their own food. Many preppers have "survival vegetable gardens" where they grow produce they eat every day. But at the same time, that garden will be part of what helps them to survive for the long term.

CHOOSING WHERE TO SURVIVE

It may sound a bit strange; but one of the biggest survival questions to answer is where you are going to survive. I'm not talking about surviving being lost in the woods or surviving getting trapped in your car during a blizzard; I'm talking about surviving short and long-term disasters, ranging from natural disaster and social unrest, to a financial collapse or loss of the electric grid. Whether those give us advance notice or not, we still have to make a decision on where it makes the most sense for our families to survive.

On the most basic level, this question boils down to two choices – staying home and "bugging in" or leaving home, which preppers call "bugging out." But if you're going to bug out, you've really got to have someplace to go. Just bugging out and going to live in the woods is a lot harder than most people think and the survival rate is extremely low. So, you don't want to do that, unless you have no other choice.

For most of us, it makes more sense to stay at home, than it does to just pick up and leave. Most of the things we are going to do, to help our families survive, will probably be centered around our homes. They aren't necessarily things that we can take with us. Staying home and bugging in allows us to use those things to help our family survive. On top of that, our home provides shelter and contains everything we own. Leaving home means leaving a lot of that behind.

Even so, the bug in/bug out decision depends in part on how long it will be before life gets back to normal and in part on where home is and what home is. If you're living in a high-rise apartment in the center of town, you're going to have a real problem with finding resources. Besides there not being any electricity, there might not be any water either. If you don't already have a stockpile of food in your apartment (something difficult to do in an apartment), then you're going to have trouble finding food as well. These problems push you in the direction of having to leave, before you die of dehydration.

You might also be forced to abandon your home due to the disaster. When Hurricane Harvey stalled over Houston, Texas, it flooded more than 150,000 homes. No matter how well those people were prepared, they had to abandon their homes until the water went back down. Another disaster, this time a wildfire, forced the 56,000 people of Paradise, California to flee their homes, when their town burnt down, leveling all 1,200 buildings.

What this tells us is that no matter what our survival plans are, they need to include a plan for bugging out. More than anything, that means a destination that we can go to, where our families will be safe. Some such locations might be:

- **A cabin in the woods** – This is the dream of many preppers, owning a cabin in the woods, which they can set up as a survival retreat, stocking it with equipment and supplies to help their family survive any emergency. It's just a bit expensive though.

- **Friends and family** – If you have friends and family outside of your area, you might try setting up an agreement with them, where you will bug out to their home, in the case of an emergency. This would be especially good if they lived out in the country, where you could park a travel trailer and a stockpile of supplies to use.

- **Rural town** – While not quite as good an option as those first two, if you don't have anywhere else to go, you might find a rural town within a reasonable distance of your home, preferably one with a lot of abandoned buildings, and establish a cache of supplies there. Get to know some of the locals, so that they will welcome you if you show up.

- **Suburbia** – While people in suburbia might find themselves having to bug out too, that's less likely than people in the city center. Those people in the high-rises might find that a bug out to the suburbs serves them well, especially if they can establish a cache of supplies and find an abandoned building to use.

- **The wilderness** – This is a true "emergency only" option, as living off the land is extremely difficult. We have to assume that the game will be hunted out quickly; so, unless you're going to clear land and plant crops, running off into the woods isn't going to give you much of an advantage.

Ultimately, you only want to bug out if your chances of survival are going to be better bugging out, than they would be bugging in. That can change in a moment's notice; so, you want to beconstantly reviewing the situation, looking to see what's going to be better for your family. Even if you decide to bug in, the dynamics could change over time, necessitating a bug out.

DEVELOPING A SURVIVAL MINDSET

Before we get into the things you need to have, in order to survival, I want to talk about having the right mindset. This is often left off the list of "top survival priorities;" but it is the single most important one. The reason it is left off is that it is not something you can find around you; you have to find it within.

As I just said, one of the most important things you can do to survive, is to develop a positive survival mindset. This is the first thing talked about in every military survival manual I've seen; and it's first for a reason. That is, your attitude is what's going to give you the necessary motivation to do the things you need to do, in order to survive. People with the right attitude survive and those without it usually die.

There are countless examples of this, outside of the kind of survival we're talking about. Oncologists know that one of the most important factors in cancer patient survival rates is the patient's attitude. They can't fully explain why that is so, but they see it every day.

Similar to that, a survival mindset affects the survival rate of police officers who are shot in the line of duty. Those who think that they are going to die if they are shot, usually die, even if the wound is not normally life-threatening. On the flip side of that coin, those who are convinced that they are going to live will often survive through life-threatening injuries.

In simple terms, this is referred to as the "will to live." It's a very individual thing, where people decide whether they are going to live or die. It's a bit of an optimist/pessimist thing, although it goes deeper than that. But it really boils down to those who are convinced they are going to survive, will do the things they need to, in order to survive. Those who think they are going to die, may not even try to survive.

The fact that you're reading this book shows me that you're probably part of the first group. You're not one to just accept that you have to lay down and die. You want to learn what you need to do in order to survive and you're already at least somewhat motivated to do what you are going to learn.

The things you are going to learn in this book, plus the skills that you will continue to work on, after reading this book, are all going to help boost your confidence. That's important too. Going back to looking at the military again, we find that the one thing that makes elite troops into elite troops is their training. There is no super soldier formula; but there's a lot of super soldier training going on in the world's militaries.

That training makes those soldiers more effective; but it also makes them believe that they are more effective. That belief is often the critical difference between them defeating the other guy and surviving and them becoming the victim of the other guy.

Putting that into our context, the more survival skills you learn, the more confident you will be that you will survive. That alone will push you to do things that you may not have thought possible. When the time comes to apply your skills, you won't just lay down and die; you'll do whatever you can to survive and to make sure your family survives as well.

Don't get me wrong; survival is a challenging task, especially in the wake of a disaster. It can often be harder to survive the aftermath of a disaster, than it can be to survive the disaster itself. But it is not an insurmountable impossibility, especially for those who are trained and who have a positive mental attitude about their own ability to survive.

YOUR MOST IMPORTANT SURVIVAL NEEDS

Surviving a disaster can be extremely complicated. One of the keys to make it possible is to make sure that you know what your priorities are. That may sound simple, but modern society has us so far removed from the basics of survival, that most people don't know what they are. If they can come up with any answer at all, other than to say "My phone, my keys and my credit card," it will probably be "food, clothing and shelter." But while all of those are important to our survival, the answer is still wrong. It leaves out one key ingredient, while only giving two-thirds of another.

So, just what are our most important survival needs?

• **#1 Maintaining Our Core Body Temperature** – While the human body can survive a wide range of environmental conditions, it can only survive within a very narrow window of core body temperature.

If our core temperature rises or falls only a few degrees, it severely impedes our ability to think. A few degrees more and we will die.

- **#2 Clean Drinking Water** – Our bodies contain a huge amount of water, with water being part of countless chemical reactions every second. Without sufficient water, we begin to dehydrate and those chemical reactions stop, leading to our death. But the water that we drink needs to be clean; that basically means being clean of microscopic pathogens that can cause dysentery or other disease.

- **#3 Food** – While nowhere near as important as water, our next priority is having food to eat, providing our bodies with the energy they need to function, building blocks for making more cells, and other nutrients that are all part of the massive number of chemical reactions that happen in our bodies every day.

These three are often expressed in the survival community through the "Rule of 3s." There are various versions of this, but with the time varying, but the relationship between the times remains roughly the same. This rule states: "You can only life 30 minutes without maintaining your core body temperature (some say three hours), three days without clean water, and 30 days without food" (again, the amount of time you can live without food might vary, but 30 at least contains a 3).

There are three other things that I would like to add to this list; because at any one moment in time, they can actually jump up to the number one slot. The reason they aren't there already, is that they aren't always needed. But we need to be aware of them and prepared to take care of those needs at any time. They are:

- **#4 Fire** – We use fire for a wide variety of things, including keeping warm, cooking our food, providing light, comfort and protecting ourselves from wild animals.

- **#5 First-Aid** – Injuries can kill and the kinds of injuries which are associated with a disaster are usually serious ones. On top of that, medical services can be difficult to get to and overloaded once you get there. Being able to treat wounds can save the life of a family member.

- **#6 Self-Defense** – Sadly, disasters cause the two-legged predators in any society to come out of the woodwork, where they prey on ordinary people. With the chance that law-enforcement will be overloaded, or in the worst possible scenarios, might abandon their posts to care for their own families, we need to be able to take care of ourselves.

In the following chapters, we are going to go into a much more in-depth discussion about these six areas, followed by a discussion about how to prepare for and execute an effective bug out. My intent in this book is to provide you with the information that you need to have, in order to survive.

CHAPTER ONE:

#1 PRIORITY MAINTAINING YOUR CORE BODY TEMPERATURE

The human body is an amazing machine; but it has its limits. One key limitation is that it needs to be at a certain temperature to operate properly. If that temperature rises just a few degrees (hyperthermia) or drops just a few degrees (hypothermia) the brain has trouble thinking clearly, the muscles struggle to operate properly and even things like food digestion don't appen as smoothly as they should. It doesn't take long for the body to begin shutting down. A few more degrees higher or lower and the body stops working altogether.

While these two conditions are equally dangerous, hypothermia, the loss of body heat, is the big killer. If someone is suffering from hyperthermia, they will likely die of dehydration, sweating out too much of the body's water. But hyperthermia can actually set in, without the afflicted person realizing what's happening to them.

It can be easy to think that hypothermia is something that only happens in the wintertime; but that's not true. Our body's core temperature is about 98.6°F. So, any time that the ambient temperature is lower than that, we are radiating heat. If we fall in the river, getting our clothes wet or even sweat too much, we accelerate this process of radiating heat. Wet clothes don't provide insulation (other than wool), but rather cause us to lose body heat ever faster than being naked. The colder the temperature, the faster we lose our body heat.

Obviously, it is dangerous to fall in a river in the middle of the winter, but it can be equally dangerous to fall in that river just before sundown, in the summertime, when the temperature starts dropping quickly. Either way, we lose heat and face the potential of losing too much heat, too fast.

To combat this risk to our lives, we use three things: shelter, clothing and fire. In this chapter we're going to discuss the first two of those and we'll talk about fire in a later chapter.

WHAT SHELTER AND CLOTHING DO FOR US

The main purpose of shelter is to protect us from the weather, especially wind and rain. A roof over our heads keeps the rain off of our bodies and our clothing, helping to ensure that we don't lose body heat too fast. Walls help in that they block the wind, as wind will make us colder, by removing the bubble of warm air that our body produces around itself. At the same time, if our clothing is wet, that wind will cause the water to evaporate faster, by presenting dry air all the time. In order to evaporate, the water will absorb heat from the nearest possible place... our bodies.

Modern homes add one more thing to that more classic understanding of shelter, in that we build them with heating and air conditioning systems in them. In the past, only heating was available and that existed only in rooms where the fireplace or wood-burning stove was located. Cooling only came by a breeze or by the artificial breeze caused by a fan.

To help with the efficiency of heating and cooling our homes, the walls and attic are insulated. This insulation provides hundreds of layers of air pockets. Temperature travels slowly through those layers, as each needs to be warmed, before it can warm the next layer. The more layers, the longer this process takes, holding in or out more heat.

Clothing works as a portable shelter. Depending on the type of clothing, it can protect against rain, wind and/or temperature extremes. Of course, the right clothing is needed to protect the wearer under any particular circumstances. A rain poncho is great to protect from the rain, but won't do much to keep someone warm on a cold day.

YOUR HOME AS A SURVIVAL SHELTER

If we assume that a disaster is going to happen sometime and our number one choice is to stay home, bugging in, rather than bugging out; then it only makes sense to ensure that our home is the best possible survival shelter. But just how do we do that?

Based upon the description above of what a shelter is supposed to do, probably the most important thing to do is to make sure that our homes are in good repair. Weather-related natural disasters can be hard on the home, breaking windows, tearing off roof shingles, causing tree limbs to break off and fall on the roof, puncturing it, and causing other damage. The first part of any home which will be damaged in such a storm is anything that is loose or overshadowed by a tree. That means loose shingles and shutters are a danger.

When it comes to hurricanes, the wind pressure may very well be strong enough to break window glass. Windows are rated for a particular design pressure (DP).

Common windows have a DP of 15, which corresponds to a wind speed of about 77 mph being able to break them. The strongest windows have a DP of 50, which is good for winds of 177 mph. But windows aren't marked with this rating; so unless you installed them or had them installed, you have no way of knowing what the rating is.

To counter strong winds, it's advisable to install working shutters on the house or to cut pieces of plywood, at least 5/8" thick, to install over the windows during a hurricane. There are spring clips that can be used in many cases, which press against the inside of the window frame, eliminating the need to drill holes in the siding for screws.

The other thing to look at in the home itself is its insulation. Poorly insulated homes will lose heat faster. That results in higher energy bills during normal times; but should another winter storm Uri come, as did in February of 2021, the quality of the home's insulation becomes a factor in survival.

Typically, the biggest problem is the insulation in the attic. Not only is it often installed in a way that leaves gaps; but it crushes down over time, reducing the R-value of the insulation. For a few hundred dollars, you can buy 10 bales of blown-in insulation and the home improvement center where you buy it will rent you the machine to blow it in for free. A few hours work will allow you to greatly improve the insulation value of your home's attic, preparing it for that next survival scenario.

Besides these things, there are other projects, like rainwater capture, gardening, and improving your home's security which you should consider. We will discuss these later on in the book.

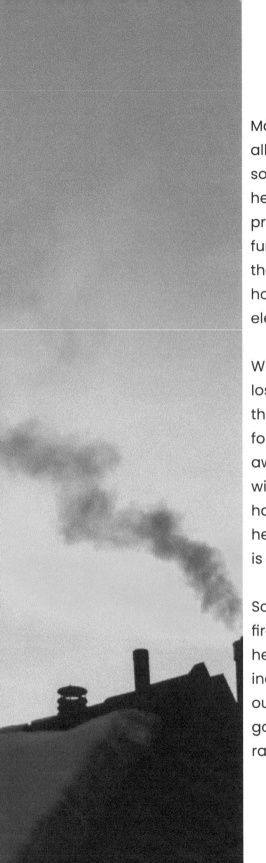

HEATING YOUR HOME WHEN THERE IS NO POWER

Modern home heating systems all require electricity to operate; so there's a good chance that the heating will go out in our homes in pretty much any disaster. Gas-fired furnaces still need electricity for the controls and blower and even hot water heating systems require electricity for the pump.

Without electrical power, our homes lose their heating capability. While the insulation will hold the heat in for a while, it will eventually radiate away from the home, leaving us without heat. To prevent that from happening, we need an alternate heat source, for use when the power is down.

Some homes have a built-in fireplace, which will supply some heat. But fireplaces are notoriously inefficient, with more heat radiating out the back of the fireplace and going up the chimney than is radiated into the room.

That's why the wood-burning stove was invented. By bringing the fire into the room, instead of having it along an outside wall, the stove is able to radiate heat in all directions, from both the stove itself and the chimney pipe.

Installing a wood-burning stove in a single-story home is fairly easy. A heath needs to be built for the stove to set on. This hearth must be at least ½" thick of fireproof material, extending at least 12" to the front of the stove and six inches to either side. The stove must be at least 18" from the walls and any furniture needs to be kept at least three feet from the front of it. As for the chimney, single wall pipe can be used up to the ceiling, allowing it to radiate heat; but from there on up through the roof it must be double or triple wall. Check your local building codes for which.

Another nice thing about a wood-burning stove is that it can be installed temporarily in an emergency, running the chimney out through a window. To do that, one window pane needs to be removed and a piece of aluminum flashing cut to fill in the gap between the stove pipe and the window frame. On the outside of the home, the chimney must go at least three feet above the roof.

Avoid the wood-burning stoves that use wood pellets, if it is being bought for survival purposes. Free wood is actually fairly easy to come by, if you're willing to invest a little elbow grease. Offer to cut dead limbs, fallen limbs and dead trees around your neighborhood or town. There are plenty of people who would love to have that service for free and will be even more happy when you offer to haul off the wood.

Two other heating options are worth considering for short-term survival: propane and kerosene. Neither of these require a hearth; although it is a good idea to keep flammable materials from making contact with the heaters. There are portable heaters made using both of these types of fuels. The real question becomes which fuel is more readily available where you live. Propane is available just about anywhere, but kerosene isn't. It is used as a heating fuel in the north, so it is readily available there; but it is almost impossible to find in the south.

One problem with any of these emergency heat sources is that they really only heat one room; the room they are located in. So your family is going to have to do a sleepover in the living or family room, wherever the heat source is located. That's an inconvenience, but at least you'll be warm.

FINDING SHELTER IN THE WILD

If you decide to bug out, you're going to need someplace to stay, wherever you go. Assuming that's out in the wild somewhere, you probably won't be able to find an abandoned building to use, although you might find an abandoned mine in some parts of the country. Be careful about abandoned mines and don't go very far inside. Some are safe, but others are very unstable. It's hard to tell which is which.

Most preppers do not bother carrying a tent when bugging out; but I highly recommend it. Be sure to buy the lightest backpacking tent you can find that is big enough for your family. Having a good tent means that you can set up camp in minutes, rather than spending over an hour to build a shelter.

But what if you don't have a tent? Then you're either going to have to find what's available in nature or build something with what nature provides. You'll want to stop a good two hours before sunset, in order to establish camp, gather firewood and start a fire and build a shelter.

If you don't have a watch, you can tell how much time you have available till sunset by holding your hand horizontally on the horizon, at arm's length. Each finger of distance the sun is above the horizon equals 15 minutes. So you should stop when the sun's distance above the horizon is equal to the fingers of both hands. Start looking for a good campsite before that, preferably one that offers some natural shelter. What sorts of shelter?

- **Cave** – look out for previous residents

- **Rock outcropping** – can provide walls, with a tarp over the top for a roof

- **Overhanging embankment** – be cautious if it is raining; the same watercourse that cut the embankment might fil up again

- **Small clearing** in the center of a thicket of trees

- **Upturned deadfall** – the root mass makes a rather solid wall and the trunk and branches can provide overhead cover

- **Big pine tree** – the branches of some large pine trees will brush the ground; but those branches will connect to the trunk three to four feet off the ground, leaving a space underneath them. Any branches remaining in that area will be dead and dry, making them usable for firewood

Keep in mind that you may not find a perfect shelter; but rather only a partial shelter. Still, that will save you time and effort, cutting down the amount of work required to finish off the job.

BUILDING A SURVIVAL SHELTER

If no shelter is readily available, you're going to need to build one. It's a good idea to keep a tarp in your bug out bag or other pack for this, even if you don't carry a tent. Even a rain poncho will work. Pick one of the ultralight tarps or ponchos, made to save weight for backpackers.

The classic wilderness shelter is a lean-to. This consists of a tree limb suspended horizontally between two trees, attached to them about three feet off the ground. Sticks are leaned against this, tying them at the top and allowing the bottom to sit on the ground, anchoring them there with dirt or rocks. A tarp can be used to cover this, but usually branches are cut from trees and leaned against the framework, with the leaves pointed down to shed rain.

One of the more popular survival shelters is what is known as a "debris
hut." This is a one-person shelter, made by leaning a tree limb against a standing tree,

and tying it there at about three feet off the ground. The other end of the limb sets on the ground. Then take sticks and lean them against this pole, every couple of inches apart, making an equilateral triangular cross section that is wider at the tree end and gets smaller as it goes toward the ground end. Finally, pile a whole bunch of leaves and other debris off the forest floor onto this framework to insulate it and keep rain out. The resulting space inside the hut is cozy and can be rather warm.

For a larger shelter, find a small clearing with a number of saplings forming a rough circle. Other samplings inside that circle might have to be removed; then the saplings that are forming the hut can be brought together at the top and tied, making a dome. The saplings removed can then be tied to these, going around the circle in horizontal rings. Finally, branches are cut and layered on this framework, from the bottom up, with the leaves pointing down to shed water.

CHAPTER TWO:

#2 PRIORITY CLEAN WATER TO DRINK

With our bodies being comprised of more water than anything else, the potential for dehydration is a very real risk that must be considered. But here's the rub; our bodies naturally expel water, in the form of urine and perspiration, as part of the body's normal operation. So it's not like we can conserve the water in our bodies, we need to be constantly replacing it. If we can't do that, it causes a host of medical problems.

On the flip side of that coin, we have to take care that the water we are drinking is not bringing anything harmful into our bodies. There's a long list of harmful substances that can come into our bodies through water, such as chemicals and radiation; but the biggest concern is microscopic pathogens; bacteria, viruses and protozoa that can cause us to become ill.

Some of the bacteria that are harmful to us when drunk with our water are already found in our bodies,

specifically in the intestines. There, those bacteria are useful; but if those same bacteria get into our stomach, they end up causing gastrointestinal distress and dysentery, dehydrating us through diarrhea.

The only way that we can remain safe is to assume that all water is unsafe, during a time of crisis. That means treating all water found in the great outdoors as suspect; but it also means distrusting the water coming out of our faucet... at least until we are told be competent authority that the water has been tested and is safe to drink.

But an even bigger problem may exist; that of finding water at all. Without power, our municipal water treatment plants can't operate for long. They are required to have diesel generators and a stock of fuel on-hand; but as we saw in Texas, during Winter Storm Uri, that isn't always enough. The generators didn't run, due to the cold weather, and so most of the state was without running water for five days.

STORING WATER

Most survival instructors will tell us that we need a gallon ofwater per person, per day, for drinking and cooking. But if you're in a hot climate, you can sweat our more than that in a day. Besides that, we use water for a host of other needs, especially cleaning. A munch more realistic figure would be five gallons of water per person, per day, as a minimum, which is still only about 1/10 of what we typically use. Out of that, only about a gallon actually needs to be what is known as "potable water," water that is safe to drink.

Ensuring that we have enough water and especially enough cleandrinking water during a time of crisis requires that we take a multi-level approach to the problem. To start with, we need to stockpile water. Starting with the five gallons per day figure, we can readily see that we need 20 gallons per day for a family of four. That works out to 140 gallons per week and 600 gallons per month. That's a lot of purified water to store.

It would cost a small fortune to buy that much bottled water to keep on-hand for emergencies. Fortunately, we don't have to. While it makes sense to keep a couple of cases of purified water on-hand, most of our water stockpile can be in other containers, such as cleaned out gallon milk jugs and 55-gallon plastic drums.

So, just how much water should we stockpile? That's a hard one to answer, as we have no idea of how long we might be without municipal water in the event of a disaster. With that in mind, my attitude is "the more the merrier."

All we need is a way to store it.

Probably the best stealth water tank you can get is an above-ground swimming pool. Not only do they hold a lot of water; but nobody is going to see that pool as a water cistern. Yet, the chemicals we need to put in that pool to keep the water safe for swimming are the same ones that we need to put in there to keep it safe to drink. When a disaster strikes, we can use that water with confidence and in the meantime, the kids can enjoy the pool.

FINDING WATER NEAR YOUR HOME

Should the municipal water authority stop pumping clean water to your home, there are still options available to you, over and above what you've got stored. To start, there's the water in your hot water heater and the home's plumbing pipes. You can get the water out of the hot water heater, by connecting a hose to the drain valve, located near the bottom of the heater. Just make sure that you shut off power and/or gas to the heater, before emptying it.

You can get the water out of your home's pipes at the hot water heater, if the hot water heater is located in the basement. Most hot water heaters have threaded fittings for the water outlets, allowing them to be removed and the water to be drained out. If your home doesn't have a basement, locate the toilet that is at the lowest elevation and find the water valve on the wall that fills the toilet tank. Disconnect the hose from the toilet tank and drain the water out into a container. It can be helpful to open the faucets upstairs, or in other parts of the house, to facilitate the water flowing out this opening.

Obviously, the water in your pipes and hot water heater isn't going to last long, so you're going to need to range farther afield in your search for water. If you happen to have a fountain or landscaping pond on your property, those can be good sources of water as well; but for most of us, we're going to have to look off-site to find water. Some possible places for that are:

- Local municipal or school swimming pools

- Rivers and streams

- Irrigation canals

- Ponds and lakes

- Landscaping ponds and fountains at government businesses and office buildings

If you carry a four-way silcock key with you, as you search for water, you can use it to drain the pipes of commercial buildings of water. This tool will allow you to open the outside hose spigot, draining whatever water is in the building. That can amount to a considerable amount of water in multi-floor commercial buildings.

It's a good idea to locate these potential water sources before a disaster strikes and annotate them on a map. That way, you won't have to waste time and energy looking for them after the disaster strikes.

HARVESTING WATER FROM NATURE

Regardless of which resources are available near your home, your best source of water is to be able to harvest it right there on your own property. That either means drilling a well or rainwater capture. While a well is the more secure and reliable means of getting water, it is also considerably more expensive, as that usually requires hiring a well-drilling contractor to do the job. There are ways of doing shallow wells yourself, but the best water comes from deep wells.

Rainwater capture is much easier and cheaper, although it is dependent on rainfall. If you live in a part of the country which receives abundant rainfall, that's not much of an issue; but if you live in a more arid part of the country, it can be problematic. You might actually get enough rainfall to survive on; but it all comes in two or three months, leaving you long dry spells in-between time.

Storing enough water to get through till the next rainfall could require that swimming pool or some other large cistern.

It's actually quite amazing how much water you can harvest from rainfall. I live in a fairly arid part of the country, and I get enough rainwater off of only part of my roof, that if I had enough storage, it could provide all our needs, during a time of crisis.

Rainwater capture basically means collecting and saving the water that is running off your home's roof. If you've already got gutters and downspouts, you've got half of what you need to make that a reality. All that you need is something to capture the water that's coming out of the downspout. That normally means some sort of rain barrel.

While you can buy commercially manufactured rain barrels and attach them to your downspouts, a more budget friendly option is to buy used blue plastic barrels. Just make sure that the barrels you get are thoroughly cleaned out, as those barrels are used to transport chemicals.

For a larger water storage capacity, you can attach multiple barrels together with PVC plumbing pipe and fittings. The only tricky thing about that is going through the side or bottom of the barrel. Those barrels are blow molded, so the walls of the barrel are not of even thickness. Chances are high that you'll need a thick rubber seal to go along with the fitting. I've used 2" drains in the bottom of the barrels before, with the thick rubber seal that's used between a toilet tank and bowl to keep it from dripping.

Another option is to use an IBC (intermediate bulk container). These square plastic containers hold either 275 or 330 gallons and are encaged in square aluminum tubing, with an integral pallet. They give you more water storage in a smaller footprint, increasing your water supplies. As with the barrels, it's important to ensure that the inside of the IBC is clean, so that the chemicals that were in it don't contaminate your water.

A little trick to keep mosquitoes from breeding in your rainwater collection cistern is to buy a couple of goldfish at the pet store and put them in the cistern or barrel. The goldfish will eat the mosquito larvae, effectively ending them as a threat.

FINDING WATER IN THE WILD

So far, we've talked about finding water either at your home or near your home; but what if you're forced to bug out? How can you find water in the wild?

To start with, I'd make sure you have topographical maps of the area you live in, the area you would be bugging out to and everywhere in-between. Topographical maps will show all naturally-occurring and man-made water sources, although they will not show ranchers' water tanks or the swimming pools in people's back yards. They'll even show intermittent sources of water, such as streams that only run after a rainfall.

But what if you don't have a topographical map? You can still find water. There are three basic steps involved:

- **Go downhill** – Regardless of where you are, if you go far enough downhill, you'll eventually find water. The only real question is how soon you'll find it. That depends on the contour of the land, how arid it is and when the last rainfall was. Nevertheless, regardless of where you are, you're best off going downhill in your search for water.

- **Look for green** – Plants need water even more than we do, so one of the surest signs of water is areas where plants are growing more densely. That doesn't necessarily mean that you'll find surface water where you find those plants though. The water might be hidden underground and need to be dug up.

- **Follow animals** – Most animals water at dawn and dusk. So if you see animals moving close to those times, then it's likely that they're either moving towards water or away from it. Animal trails are a good sign as well, with most of them leading to water, especially if they go downhill.

In arid climates, expect to have to do some digging. Look for areas of dried mud in low-lying areas, especially where there is shade. Most likely those were the last areas to dry up and there will still be water underground. Dig a hole and allow water to seep into it.

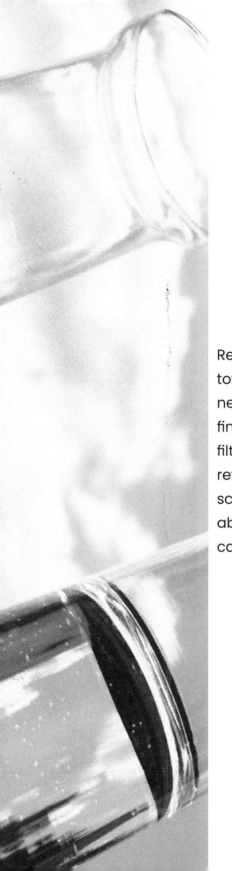

PURIFYING WATER

Regardless of whether you are in town or in the wild, you're going to need to purify any water that you find. That means more than just filtering out dirt and silt, it mostly refers to eliminating those microscopic pathogens we were talking about earlier. There are three basic categories of ways to go about this:

FILTRATION

Filtration is just as it sounds, using a filter to remove unwanted contaminants from the water. But not all filters will remove the microscopic pathogens we're concerned about. To remove bacteria requires a filter that is rated for 0.2 microns. Whole house filters, faucet filters and some others are sediment filters that don't filter down that fine. Nevertheless, there are a number of excellent filters on the market, which will filter out bacteria. One sure sign, when shopping for filters, is to look for one that says it "Removes 99.99% of all bacteria."

For home you're going to need something that filters at least a few gallons a day, such as one that uses a five-gallon bucket as its water source. The two best brands for this are the Berkey system and the Sawyer filter. The Berkey also removes some radiation and chemicals from the water.

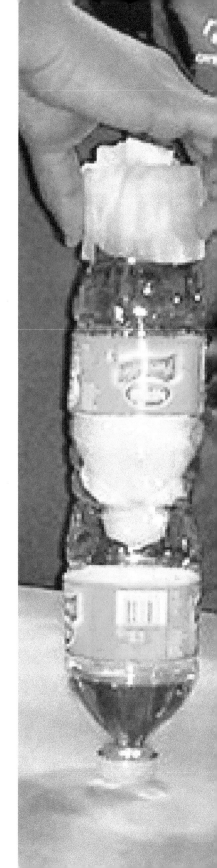

For bugging out you're going to need something much more portable. Each family member should have a straw-type water filter, such as the Lifestraw or one of the knockoffs to that brand. You'll also need a bag-type filter system, which will allow you to filter water to fill canteens and water bottles.

Reverse Osmosis

Reverse osmosis is a sub-category of filtration; at least for our purposes. Technically it isn't a means of filtration, but it is close enough to appear the same from a survival viewpoint. The water produced by reverse osmosis is generally purer than that produced by filtration.

Doing reverse osmosis requires two things: a reverse osmosis membrane canister and a pump. The membrane usually comes as part of a reverse osmosis unit, which will also include sediment filters. Filtering out the sediment, before the water gets to the membrane, helps ensure that the membrane lasts as long as possible.

The issue with reverse osmosis, from a survival point of view, is the pump. Water going through the system has to be put under enough pressure to force the clean water through the membrane. This usually means using an electric pump, which might not be possible during a time of crisis, when the power is out. However, there are some manual pumps which can do the job as well, making it possible to purify water with a reverse osmosis unit even in times of crisis.

CHEMICAL PURIFICATION

Along with filtration, chemical purification is the number one thing that municipal water authorities use for purifying our water. They use chlorine as the main chemical for purification. We can find that in normal household bleach; not the scented kind or the color safe kind, but just generic laundry bleach.

To purify water with chlorine bleach, put eight drops of water per gallon into the water. Mix it up and allow it 20 minutes to sit. The chlorine will kill the microscopic pathogens, making the water safe to drink. If you don't like the chlorine smell in your water, allow it to sit uncovered, overnight. That will allow the chlorine to evaporate, leaving behind the purified water.

For larger containers of water, such as barrels and IBCs, one ml of a liquid is equal to 20 drops. So for a 55 gallon drum of water, you need 22 ml of bleach. It might be a good idea to buy a graduated cylinder and keep it with your bleach supply, just for measuring it out.

By the way, adding 8 drops of bleach to each gallon of water that you're storing will help ensure that your water stockpile remains pure and ready to drink when you need it. As long as the container is sealed, the chlorine won't evaporate and will continue to keep your water pure.

HEAT PURIFICATION

As pretty much everyone knows, you can boil water to purify it. But most people don't realize that you don't need to bring the water to boiling to make it pure. A French microbiologist in the mid-1800s discovered that all you need to do is bring it up to 158°F and hold it there for no more than a minute. This process is called pasteurization, after the scientist that discovered it. It is the process that is used for purifying milk, so that we don't receive dangerous bacteria from the cows that produce that milk.

In order to pasteurize water, we need to have some means of measuring its temperature, such as a candy thermometer. Another excellent option is a WAPI (water pasteurization indicator). This simple device was developed for use in third-world countries, where purified water is hard to come by. It consists of a wax pellet in a plastic capsule. Placed in the water that is being heated, the wax capsule melts at 160°F, indicating that the water is hot enough to be pasteurized. Once the wax cools, it solidifies once again, making it ready to be re-used.

Pasteurization is beneficial in that it uses less energy than boiling. This can be important in cases where firewood and other types of fuel are hard to come by.

Distillation

Distillation is a sub-category of heat purification, one that produces the purest possible water. It works by heating the water hot enough to bring it up to boiling and then collecting the steam that is produced, condensing it back down to a liquid. Only the water will come through in this manner, leaving behind everything else. Hence, the ability for distillation to provide the purest water possible. It can even do this from seawater, removing the salt.

In order to distill water a still is needed. This consist of a sealable retort (such as a double-boiler or a pressure canner) where the water is heated up to boiling, a copper tube which acts as a condenser and a container to capture the purified water produced by the still. The copper tube needs to flow downhill, as quickly after exiting the retort as possible and continue flowing downhill along its entire length. This is most easily accomplished by making the tube into a spiral or funnel shape.

The only other thing that is needed for a still to work is heat. This normally comes from a wood fire, but can actually come from any available source, just as long as it heats the water higher than 212°F. Be sure to keep the fire going, other than to stop and refill the retort with water.

CHAPTER THREE:

#3 PRIORITY FOOD FOR THE BODY

In a way, food might seem a distant third, when compared to shelter and water; but it is the next survival priority. Depending on whose numbers you use, we humans can survive from 30 to 100 days without food. But the key word in that sentence is "survive." Survival means we aren't dead; but it doesn't necessarily mean that we are functioning the way that we should. Lack of proper food for even a few days will start to affect our energy levels, coordination and attention.

Granted, there are those of us who are carrying a lot of spare energy, stored up in our bodies. But depending only on that can be dangerous, as all it does is provide energy; it doesn't provide protein. Without sufficient protein in our diets, our bodies will literally cannibalize healthy cells, in order to get the proteins necessary to build new cells.

Nutritionists and personal trainers will tell you that trying to lose body fat too quickly is dangerous, as it causes the type of cannibalization I was just talking about. We want to keep ourselves eating, even when in a survival situation. But just what do we need to eat?

Assuming we have time to prepare and are able to stockpile some food, a survival diet needs to focus on the three main macronutrients. We can ignore the micronutrients (the stuff all the nutritionists love to talk about) for about 30 days. But in a long-term survival situation, we need to bring them back into our diet, in order to maintain our health. So, what are these macronutrients?

- **Carbohydrates** – Carbs are the main energy source for our bodies; easily broken down into simple sugars, which provide energy for our muscles. A survival diet needs to be a good 60% to 70% carbohydrates.

- **Fats** – Like carbs, fats are also broken down into simple sugars; but it takes longer. This allows the energy from fats to arrive later, giving us a second wind. Fats should compromise 15% to 25% of a survival diet.

- **Proteins** – As I've already mentioned, proteins are needed for building new cells. The best place to get them from is meat, poultry and fish. We should strive to maintain 10% of our diet as proteins, both from plants and animals, as part of our survival diet.

The other thing we should keep in mind, along with this, is that in a survival situation we're probably going to be eating a whole lot less than we do now. Most Americans eat too much and even the government figures of 2,000 to 2,500 calories a day may be a bit too much, especially in a survival situation.

Even if you have plenty of food to eat, it's not wise to keep eating like normal in a survival situation, while everyone around you is starving. If everyone else is losing weight, due to lack of food, and you look plump and happy, it's going to make people suspicious. Eventually some of those people are going to come around, looking to see what you've got stored in your home… and they won't ask nicely and be friendly when they do so.

STOCKPILING FOOD FOR EMERGENCIES

One of the things that the prepping community is most known for is stockpiling food and other supplies. As we all saw during the COVID-19 pandemic, it doesn't take much to mess up our supply chain, emptying the stores of food. Having food on-hand, in case an emergency hits that shuts down the stores, shuts down our ability to buy with plastic or shuts down the ability for our nation's trucking fleet to get food to the stores, we need food that we can eat.

The first question that brings up is just how much food should we have?

To be honest, there is no real answer to that question, because none of us can see into the future, allowing us to know what sort of disaster we're going to face and how long it is going to last. We've got to go with our best guess; so figure out the worst scenario you expect to encounter and now long that will last and then double it. That's how much food you should have.

Granted, you probably won't be able to run out today and buy that much food. That's your target; something that you're going to work towards. Most of us have to buy the food for our stockpiles bit by bit, working our way up to our goal. Use sales and buying in bulk whenever possible, but other than that, keep your purchase levels even, so that the various items in your stockpile will last roughly the same amount of time. In other words, work to buy a month's worth of food, and then add another month's worth, rather than buying six months' worth of one item.

The second question that naturally comes up is what sorts of food to stockpile?

Before the pandemic, I would have said to only stockpile non-perishable foods, based on the understanding that the electric grid would be likely to go down in just about any disaster. But 2020 and 2021 laid waste to that understanding. We went through disaster after disaster and through that whole time I only lost power for a few hours. If we lose the grid, I might lose it all; but what we've experienced is losing the meat from the grocery store shelves, without losing the grid. Besides, if the power goes out, I can always smoke, can or dehydrate that meat.

Don't get me wrong; I'm not saying that stuffing my freezer full of meat has replaced anything else in my stockpile. It hasn't. All I've done is add frozen meat to the rest of my list. So, what's the rest of that list? It consists of non-perishable foods like:

- Grains (I prefer whole grains, as they store better; but you've got to have a mill to grind them)

- Pasta in various forms (besides spaghetti, almost anything can be turned into a casserole)

- Rice (white rice seems to store better for long periods of time)

- Dry beans (great source of protein)

- Baking supplies – baking powder, baking soda, powdered milk, powdered eggs

- Cooking oil

- Peanut butter (great source of protein, as well as being a comfort food)

- Jams & jellies (to go with the peanut butter)

- Canned fruit

- Canned meats

- Canned vegetables

- Jerky (can be reconstituted in soup)

- Freeze-dried meat (can also be reconstituted in soup)

- Spaghetti sauce (anything, with spaghetti sauce on it, tastes like spaghetti)

- Cream of mushroom soup (for making casseroles)

- Spices (to make road kill and other interesting fare taste better)

- Soup starter (soup is the basic survival food, because it can be made out of anything)

- Salt (for seasoning and preserving food; we need salt in our diet to survive)

- Sugar and/or honey (sugar, like salt, is a natural preservative)

- Dried fruit

- Dried vegetables (can be reconstituted for soups, if you have a dehydrator to make them)

- Breakfast cereal

- Coffee and/or tea

Please note that this list may not be 100% complete. There are other
things that you can add; but avoid adding junk food and foods that don't have any nutritional value. Your space and your money are limited, so use them wisely.

One problem with stockpiling all that food is that a lot of it is not packaged for long-term storage. Canned goods are about the only thing we find in our grocery stores, which comes from the factory ready to sit on our shelves for 20 years or more. Just ignore the "use by" date stamped on the can. Unless something happens to damage that can, the food inside will stay good for years. I've seen 80-year-old canned goods which were still good to eat.

But canning only works for wet foods, not dry foods. While there are people experimenting with what is known as "dry canning," it hasn't been around long enough to be sure that it will work for the long term. So, what do we do with all the dry foods mentioned in that list? We have a way of packaging them.

You'll need:

- 6-gallon aluminized Mylar bags

- Food grade 5-gallon buckets

- Permanent marker

- Oxygen absorbers

- Hair straightener

- Vacuum cleaner with hose

- Rubber mallet

- A lot of food

To package the food:

1. Start by opening the aluminized Mylar bags and inserting them into the buckets.

2. Fill each bag/bucket with one kind of food, stopping about an inch from the top of the bucket.

3. Mark the outside of the bucket, in several places, to show what's in it.

4. Using the hair straightener, seal off all of the top edge only of the bag, leaving just enough room to stick the vacuum cleaner hose in the opening.

5. Working quickly, open the package of oxygen absorbers and put one in each bag; then put just the very end of the vacuum cleaner hose in the opening, sucking out as much air as possible. Take care not to put it in far enough to suck out any food.

6. Seal the top of the bag the rest of the way with the hair straigthener.

7. Fold the flap of the bag over to lie flat in the top of the bucket and put the lid on.

8. Use the rubber hammer to drive the lid on, to the point where the seal in the lid is compressed by the rim of the bucket.

Please note that the oxygen absorbers are very fast-acting. You might want to have an assistant for this process, just to deal with the oxygen absorbers. The idea is to get them out of their shipping bag and into the food bags as quickly as possible, sealing off the bag so that they don't have a chance to pull oxygen out of the room's air.

GROWING YOUR OWN FOOD

Many experienced preppers have taken to growing as much of their own food as they can. You've probably seen an article sometime about a family who was growing all their own food in their backyard. I had a neighbor once like that and it was surprising how much food he could grow.

There was actually a time when growing your own food was commonplace. Even as late as World War II, the government was encouraging people to plant "victory gardens" to grow their own food, so that the food from the farms could be sent to the military. While some things are a bit harder to grow, it is fairly easy to grow most vegetables and even some fruits.

Growing in raised beds is preferable to growing in the ground, as you can get a better yield out of your garden. Part of this is that plants can be planted closer together in a planter box than in the ground,

but the bigger reason is that in building planting boxes you end up having to bring in good potting soil to fill the beds. The soil is actually the most important part of any garden, as it provides the nutrients to the plants, as well as being the way that water gets to the plant's roots.

There are a couple of major things to consider when preparing to start growing your own food. The first of these is the growing zone that you're living in. The USDA (US Department of Agriculture) has broken the country down into 10 growing zones, based upon the climate and temperature. This is shown on a map, which can be found all over the place online. Some plants need a cooler climate, while others need a warmer one. So you'll need to pick plants to grow, which match the growing zone you live in.

The second major consideration is the type of seed you buy. Today, we have three options available to us:

- **GMO** – Genetically modified seed. These are seed created in a lab, in order to bring out certain characteristics, such as the size of the fruit and the timing for harvest. But the seed from GMO crops is sterile, so you can't harvest your seed and save it to plant the next year. That makes it basically useless from a survival point of view.

- **Hybrid** – Hybrid seed comes from breeding two different varieties of a plant together, like mixing two types of apples' seed, to produce a third type of apple. The seeds that comes from those apples are not sterile; but they will revert back to one of the parent varieties, which may not be as desirable.

- **Heirloom** – Heirloom seed are the old varieties which have been kept genetically the same throughout the years. While these may be a bit harder to find, there are a few organizations online, which specialize in heirloom seed. From a survival viewpoint, the big advantage of heirloom seed is that the seeds from the produce can be saved and dried for use the next year.

Besides good soil, the plants you are planting will need plenty of sunlight and water. Be sure to build your planters in places where they will not be overshadowed and establish a regular watering schedule. It's usually best to water just before sunset, as that gives the water the most time to soak into the ground, rather than being evaporated off by the sun.

In addition to planting vegetables, you might want to consider planting some fruit trees and berry bushes. These generally need more time to begin producing any edible fruit than your vegetables will, but once they do start producing, they will grow a considerable amount of food each year.

COOKING FOOD WHEN THE POWER IS OUT

Most of us are accustomed to cooking on a range in our kitchens. But if the power is out, that range probably won't be working; nor will the microwave or the conventional oven. Pretty much all those foods up there need to be cooked, so we're going to need some alternate way of cooking.

Fortunately for us, most of us already have one alternative means of cooking, although we might not think of it as a survival tool. That's our barbecue grilles. Regardless of the type of barbecue grille you may have, it can still be used for cooking on. Even if you have a gas grille and run out of gas, you can still use that grille for cooking with wood. It might damage the gas heating element, if you don't remove it; but we're talking about survival here. That heating element is replaceable, once things get back to normal.

One problem with cooking on a grille is that it can be a bit hard on the cookware. If you've got cast iron, no problem; but if you have enameled cookware, it will probably destroy the enamel on the outside of the cookware. It will still be usable; but it won't look all that good.

Perhaps a better option would be to use a camping stove. Most camping stoves today run off of small bottles of propane, which aren't all that practical for a survival situation. However, Coleman is still producing their "dual-fuel" stove, which will run off of gasoline. While gasoline might very well end up being scarce, it is more likely to be available than any other form of fuel.

Of course, if you're going to put a wood-burning stove in, there's the option of putting in a stove with a cook top. Not all wood burning-stoves have this feature, with some having the tops insulated to the point where it would be impossible to cook on them; but if you can find one that allows cooking as well, it would both solve the problem of cooking, while using the same stove for heating your home as well.

If nothing else, you can cook over a fire pit in your backyard. As long as you can find wood, you've got a means to cook with, albeit a more primitive one than you might be used to.

COOKING WITH SOLAR POWER

Some preppers have turned to the idea of using solar power for cooking. As the solar power advocates are always telling us, there's no limit to solar power and it is free. There are three basic types of solar cookers, all of which can be built at home. Obviously for any of them to work, they have to be pointed directly toward the sun. That may mean turning them slightly throughout the day.

All solar cookers work by increasing the amount of sunlight that is hitting the food pot, either by using reflectors to get more sun there or by using a magnifying glass to do so. Regardless of the type the key is to get as much sunlight striking the cooking pot as possible.

Solar Oven

The basic solar oven is a box with a glass face that is set at the right angle to point towards the sun. It works best to have the box insulated, with the inside painted flat black. That way, it can absorb as much sunlight as possible and convert it to heat. The box will also need reflectors mounted on the outside,

all the way around the glass face, to reflect more sunlight into the box. These should be about as wide as the oven itself and angled at roughly a 45 degree angle to the face of the glass.

If you're trying to make one of these quickly, a cardboard box can be used, although it will not last as long as a wood one. For the reflectors, coat cardboard panels with aluminum foil, gluing the foil down as smoothly as possible. This sort of cooker is a slow-cooker, somewhat like cooking in a Crockpot.

Parabolic Solar Cooker

A hotter cooker can be made using a parabolic reflector. To do this requires finding someone who has one of the old four-or five-foot diameter satellite antennas that you can talk them out of. Cut up small pieces of aluminum foil and paste them to the inside of the parabolic dish, shiny side up. Try to keep them as smooth as ossible for the best possible reflection.

There will be an arm sticking out in the center of the parabolic reflector, which has the actual antenna attached to it. Remove that and rig up something to hold a food pot, so that the sunlight reflected off the aluminum foil will hit that pot, heating it up. Ideally a cast iron pot should be used, but if something else is, paint it with flat black paint.

The only remaining problem is pointing the solar cooker towards the sun. Probably the easiest way to do that is to dismount the parabolic dish from the pole it is probably mounted on and set it in a large truck tire, laying on the ground. This allows the parabolic cooker to be turned and angled towards the sun.

Fresnel Solar Cooker

The most powerful type of solar cooker is made from a Fresnel Lens. That's the type of magnifying glass that's a flat sheet of plastic with concentric rings molded into the back side. If you can find one of the old type big-screen televisions on the side of the road, waiting for trash day, you can take the screen apart and use it. Either the screen itself will be a Fresnel or there will be one right behind the screen. Most of the time the bezel holding the screen in place will just pop off, but if not, it will come off easily enough with a Phillips-head screwdriver.

That lens will need to be mounted into a frame that will hold it flat. The frame will in turn need a stand that allows its angle to be adjusted, so that it can be pointed right at the sun. The focal point will be two feet behind the lens; so that's where the stand for the cooking pot should be located.

I've made this type of cooker before and I was able to fry an egg with it in a little over a minute. I've seen videos of others which got hot enough to melt a penny. A lot depends on the overall size of the Fresnel, as the bigger it is, the more sunlight it can concentrate.

FOOD IN THE WILD

A lot of people think in terms of living off the land, if they are ever forced to bug out. There's a certain romanticism about this, looking back at our nation's past, when people were able to live off the land. But things have changed considerably since then, with the nation having a much higher human population and a much smaller population of game to hunt.

For most of us, living off the land will be impossible. About the only people who could do so are those who live in less populated areas. Even then, the game is likely to get overhunted by people who have bugged out and are trying to survive.

If your plans include bugging out to the wilderness in some part of the country, then you should establish a large cache of food there, in some secure place, close to where you are planning on bugging out to. Perhaps there will be a small town nearby, which will have a storage unit that you could rent.

Probably the best chance for harvesting food from the wild in those times will be fishing. It seems that every body of water has fish in it, even though some of those might not be all that big. You can either fish with a fishing pole or for more efficient fishing, set up a trap for fish. The easiest way of making a fish trap is to pound sticks into the bottom, forming a ¾ circle. Then make an inverted funnel in the other quarter. Fish will be able to swim in through the funnel to the main body of the trap, but once inside they will be trapped, unable to find their way back out.

Another possibility is trapping small game and birds. Those won't be overhunted as fast as big game will, but they also don't provide as much meat, so you'll have to trap something every day. Nevertheless, the population of small game is greater than that of big game, making them a good option to consider. However, trapping small game though requires learning how to make traps and snares. I'd recommend getting lots of practice doing this, before you need to do it to survive.

CHAPTER FOUR:
#4 PRIORITY

FIRE – MANKIND'S OLDEST TOOL

Nobody really knows just how long mankind has used fire. Suffice it to say that the use of fire and the ability to control it were one of the first things that identified man as being different from the animals. While it might not seem so obvious to us today, fire is one of the most commonly used tools, both in our homes and in industry. We don't include it as one of the top survival priorities, but we should, as we need it for all three of the top priorities. We use it for heat, light, cooking food, protecting us from wild animals, boiling water to purify it and giving us a sense of comfort.

Yet modern man is mostly unaware of the true value of fire, because we are largely removed from the basic necessities for survival. We can see this problem manifest itself whenever someone around us tries to start a fire in their fireplace or fire pit.

Most just crumble up some newspaper and put it under a stack of logs, then keep adding newspaper until the logs finally catch fire. That's the hard way of doing things.

Fire needs three things: fuel, oxygen and heat. The fuel is the wood that we burn, which must be stacked in a way to allow good air flow, or there won't be enough oxygen. The heat comes from a match or whatever other fire starter we use. Once the fire is going, it keeps producing more heat, to keep itself burning. But getting from that first flicker of a match up to burning logs is the part that gives most people trouble. They just don't know how to do it.

HOW TO LAY A FIRE

If we want to start a fire on the first try, we need to know how to properly lay a fire. Any fire requires three stages of fuel to burn. These are:

- **Tinder** – small, dry material, which can be readily ignited with a match or spark. Examples include dry grass or moss, paper and char-cloth.

- **Kindling** – sticks the size of your finger, which can be readily ignited by the tinder

- **Fuel** – larger pieces of branches, which can be ignited by the kindling. Split wood is better, as bark protects the wood from fire.

The specific shape the fire is laid really isn't important, just as long as it allows airflow. Some people use a teepee shape, while others use a pyramid; still others do something more freeform. About the only rule,

other than airflow, is to ensure that the fire from the burning tinder can reach the kindling and the fire from the burning kindling can reach the fuel.

Since heat and therefore fire rises, it makes more sense to put the tinder at the bottom of the laid fire, with the kindling over it and the fuel over that. This means that there has to be an opening, so that you can reach in to light the tinder or to place burning tinder under the kindling.

A FEW CHOICE FIRE STARTERS

Most survival instructors will tell you that you should have two primary and two secondary forms of starting a fire. Primary means arelimited to matches and lighters. For matches, waterproof or even better, stormproof matches are preferred. While they are more expensive, they don't get ruined when they accidentally get dunked in the water.

Many people talk about using a disposable butane lighter for their other primary fire starter. But have you ever tried using one of those with even the slightest puff of wind? It's pretty much impossible, which is why I stick with one of the stormproof lighters on the market, either the electric arc ones or the ones that combine a piezoelectric striker with a refillable butane lighter. The igniter keeps reigniting the fuel, even if the wind blows it out. Keep in mind though, that in cold weather any butane lighter should be kept in your pocket, preferably inside your coat to keep it warm enough to function.

For secondary fire starters, there are many more options to choose from. The most popular is a Ferro Rod, which is a man-made mineral rod, which sparks when scraped with steel, something like using flint and steel. While this works, it's not the easiest fire starter to use. I prefer the MetalMatch, which combines magnesium, along with a Ferro Rod. A little bit of the magnesium is scraped off and then the Ferro Rod is used to ignite it. Since magnesium is highly flammable, this is a very effective fire starter.

There are also a couple of variations on the Ferro Rod that are spring-loaded, which makes them much easier to use, generating more sparks. This is my go-to secondary fire starter, especially when using it in conjunction with a fire accelerant.

A WORD ABOUT ACCELERANTS

Accelerants can be a bit confusing in the prepper and survival niche, as most venders call them "fire starters," the same term that is used for matches, lighters and Ferro Rods. But the correct term for these is actually "accelerants," the same term used for the gasoline that arsonists pour on the floor and furnishings of a building they want to burn down. While these accelerants aren't used for any nefarious purpose, they work essentially the same way.

Fire accelerants shouldn't be needed most of the time; but there are always circumstances where it is hard to start a fire and a little extra help is needed. This can be true any time the fuel being used is difficult to ignite, such as in the case of very hard hardwoods and any wood that is damp.

There are a number of commercially manufactured popular fire accelerants available, but I'll avoid plugging any particular products here. I haven't tested them all and while I'm sure of the ones I've used, there are a number which I haven't tried yet.

Mostly, I use homemade fire accelerants. The most common of these, is made of cotton balls and petroleum jelly. To make them, scoop out about a teaspoon-full of petroleum jelly, but use the back side of the spoon to scoop it out. Then using the back side of the spoon, work it into the cotton ball, being sure to get all sides and get it pressed into the cotton well. Store in an airtight container until ready to use.

An even better fire accelerant can be made out of #FFFF black powder and nail polish remover. You need the "oily nail polish remover" that contains acetone for this. Start by putting about a tablespoon of the black powder in a bowl and covering it with the nail polish remover. Allow a couple of minutes for it to soak in and then pour off the excess nail polish remover. The black powder will be softened and can be worked like putty. Roll it in a ball and knead it thoroughly, folding the putty over a good 50 times or so. The idea is to end up with a ball that has a lot of layers.

Those layers control the burn rate of the fire accelerant, which is why they are so important. This accelerant, as well as the one made with petroleum jelly, ignites easily, even with a Ferro Rod. It will burn at over 2,000°F for over 3 minutes, which is enough to dry out damp wood and ignite it.

STARTING A FIRE IN WET WEATHER

It seems we all have rather idealistic ideas about survival, especially about the weather we'll be trying to survive in. But in my experience, survival situations usually happen in bad weather, making fire starting difficult at best. Even so, we still need a fire and there are things we can do to ensure that we have one.

To start with, locate somewhere for the fire where it will be as protected from rain and wind as possible. Under a tree is good, just as long as the branches are high enough so as to be safely protected from the heat of the fire. It might be necessary to build some sort of wind break, upwind of the fire. It might also be necessary to put some rocks in the bottom of the fire pit, to keep the fire up out of the water.

The next problem is finding dry wood to burn. Some places to look include:

• Under an overhanging embankment

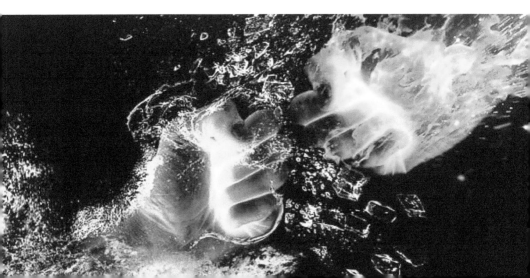

- Caves or under rock overhangs

- The underside of a deadfall

- In the midst of tightly packed forest

Keep in mind that at the worst you have fire accelerants to use, in case you have trouble starting the fire. The two I gave instructions for, especially the one made from black powder, should still be able to start the fire, even if the wood is a bit damp. Once it is started, the fire itself can be used to dry more fuel.

I avoid using those fire accelerants unless I really need them, as I want to be able to start a fire without them. Even so, I'm not shy about using them when the weather is bad. I don't feel that it harms my image as a survival expert to use a fire accelerant, any more than I feel it does to bring food with me, rather than trying to live off the land.

CHAPTER FIVE: #5 PRIORITY

FIRST-AID & PERSONAL HYGIENE

There are a couple of things that can end up superseding everything we've talked about up to this point; because when they happen, they have to be dealt with in order to survive. One of these is serious injuries and illness. We have an excellent medical community that provides us with some of the best medical care in the world; but that medical community would be hard pressed to do much of anything for us, if they didn't have medicines and electrical power.

Worse than that, if a serious enough of a disaster happens, getting to competent medical help might be a challenge. Ambulances may not be available or may be overworked so much that it would make more sense to drive injured family members in yourselves. But those ambulance drivers do more than rush people to the hospital, they provide essential first-aid and life support along the way.

Serious injuries can't wait; and there's plenty going on in most disasters to make it easy for family members to receive serious injuries. If a person is bleeding, especially if there is spurting blood, they need help right then, before they lose too much blood. If they lose more than 40% of the roughly two liters of blood in their bodies,
they'll die. But it only takes a blood loss of 14% before there are serious consequences.

Learning first aid and having the right supplies on-hand to take care of injuries, is an important part of survival. While it might not be one of the "top three priorities," when it's needed, nothing else will do.

BUILDING A FAMILY FIRST-AID KIT

an EMP would carry with them to care for patients in emergencies It's actually possible to treat wounds without having a first-aid kit on hand; but it's much faster and easier to treat them if you've got the right supplies. That means having much more than a $19.95 first-aid kit from the corner pharmacy. It means having what's known as a trauma kit; what.

You can buy trauma kits from a variety of sources; but most share one common failing. For a price of upwards of a hundred dollars, you end up with enough supplies to care for one serious injury. Then what do you do? You could spend more, buying an actual EMP trauma kit; but those aren't cheap. For the money, I prefer making my own. Not only does that allow me to stock it with enough to treat several wounds; but I can make sure I select quality medical supplies, instead of going with the low bidder.

To start with, you need some sort of case or container which will allow you to organize everything in a way that makes it easy to find. When the time comes, you don't need to be digging through a box, trying to find the right thing. There are several options you can choose from, but my favorite is a large fishing tackle box. The cantilevered trays work great for smaller items, while the large well in the bottom can hold the bigger things. Fill it full, so things can't shift around and get mixed up.

So, what do you put in that kit?

WOUND TREATMENT

- Adhesive bandages (buy the fabric ones; they're flexible and so stick better)

- Larger bandages (2"x 3", 4"x 6", etc.) (sanitary napkins work well)

- Medical tape (both adhesive and cohesive types)

- Alcohol wipes

- Clotting agent

- Antibacterial ointment (to help prevent infection)

- Gauze rolls (used primarily for packing a wound)

- Gauze pads – lots of gauze pads

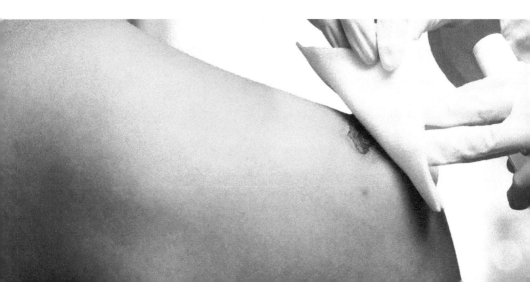

- Chest seal (for placing over a puncture to the chest cavity)

- Butterfly closures or Steri-Strips (for closing up open gashes in the skin)

- Israeli bandage or other pressure bandage

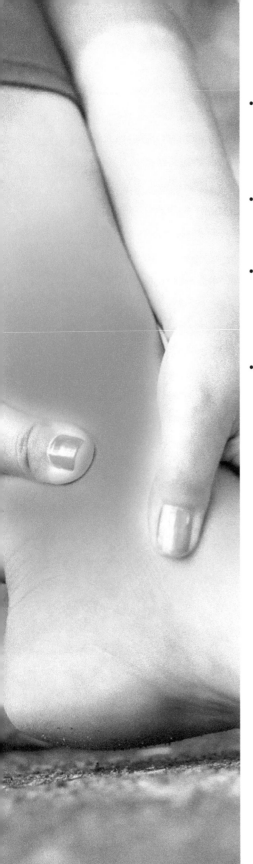

BROKEN BONES & SPRAINS

- Sam splint (a flexible aluminum splint material that can be formed to fit any limb)

- Elastic bandages (for use with the Sam splint or for sprains)

- Combat cravat (essential a triangular kerchief for use as a sling

- Instant cold packs (to help prevent swelling – must be used within 15 minutes to be effective)

PERSONAL PROTECTION EQUIPMENT

- Medical masks

- Sterile gloves

- Goggles or face shield (to protect from bodily fluids in the eyes)

- Hand sanitizer

- CPR mask

MEDICAL TOOLS

- Irrigation syringe or bottle (to flush out wounds)

- Medical scissors (made for cutting off clothing, most other scissors won't cut through seams)

- Hemostats (to clamp off arteries that are bleeding

- CAT tourniquet (the best type of tourniquet there is)

- Fine point tweezers & jeweler's loupe (for removing splinters and debris from wounds)

- Blood pressure cuff (dropping blood pressure indicates possible internal bleeding)

- Blood sugar monitor (poor diet can cause low blood sugar, which will make people's thoughts unclear, make them shaky, and make them become dizzy)

- In ear thermometer (rising temperature indicates an infection)

- Nasal pharangeal airway (a silicone tube that is inserted in the nostril and goes down to the throat. It is used for unconscious patients that might be having trouble breathing

- Needle for chest decompression (to removing air in the chest cavity but outside the lungs. A gunshot to the chest will cause the air in the lungs to come out, making it impossible to breathe unless that air is removed from the chest cavity

MEDICINES

You should stock all the standard over-the-counter medicines used in the home for treating various   ailments, especially pain relievers and antihistamines (Benadryl). In addition, I'd recommend:

- Aloe vera – for treating burns

- Hydrocortisone cream – for reducing itches from rashes

- Lidocaine – a topical anesthetic cream for temporarily numbing the skin

- Anti-diarrhea medicine

- Antibiotics

Getting antibiotics in the United States, without a prescription is basically impossible. Perhaps if you have a good relationship with your doctor, you could get them to write you a prescription for emergency antibiotics to keep on hand. Another option is to buy them in Mexico, where they can be bought over-the-counter in any pharmacy. Some preppers buy veterinary antibiotics for use, as they are essentially the same thing, just packaged under different names.

BASIC WOUND TREATMENT

Obviously, you need to know what to do with all that stuff in the first-aid kit. I realize that there are some things on that list which you probably have no idea whatsoever how to use. Unfortunately, there isn't time to go into detail on medical procedures, as this really isn't an emergency medical text. I'd recommend finding some good videos on YouTube and learning how to use them, before you need to. Nevertheless, let's talk about basic wound treatment.

Please keep in mind that I am not a medical doctor and am not giving you medical advice. The information provided below is for your edification and education. I highly recommend verifying this information and learning more than what I'm about to share.

1. Before doing anything, check the patient over to see if there are any other wounds; the one you see may not be the most life-threatening. How is the patient doing? Are they coherent? What do they say about their own condition?

2. Evaluate the wound. Is blood spurting or flowing? If it is spurting, that's an arterial bleed, which requires more serious treatment, such as packing the wound or applying a tourni-quet. If a tourniquet is applied, then mark their forehead with a large "T" to inform medical personnel to look for a tourniquet.

3. Elevate the wound to reduce blood flow. Cut away clothing, if necessary.

4. Clean the wound out to remove debris. Use clean, potable water first. Once you have removed debris, clean it with alcohol or another disinfectant.

5. Apply an antiseptic cream to help prevent infection. If you don't have any antiseptic cream, there are a variety of plants which are excellent antibiotics, such as garlic, cloves, myrrh and   turmeric.

6. If the wound is a gash, where the skin is pulled open, pull it closed to where the skin is touching and secure it there with StreiStrips or butterfly closures.

7. Cover the wound with enough absorbent bandages (gauze or cloth) to soak up the blood. Tape in place.

8.   Apply pressure to the wound to slow the bleeding and promote clot formation. If a pressure bandage is not available, use your hand or have the patient use their own hand to apply pressure.

9.   Treat to prevent shock, keeping the patient warm and the wound elevated. If the wound warrants is and especially if there was spurting blood, transport them to the nearest medical facility.

WHY PERSONAL HYGIENE IS IMPORTANT TO SURVIVAL

Some people think that personal hygiene isn't all that important, amidst all the other problems associated with survival. But nothing could be farther from the truth. Pest populations of all types tend to rise in the wake of a disaster and many of those pests are known to carry disease. In addition to that, there is the problem of human
waste disposal. Water treatment plants can become flooded, causing sewage to overflow into our rivers and streams or even our fresh water supply.

Not only do we need to keep ourselves personally clean, but we also need to keep our homes clean to help keep pests out. This can be a real challenge, at a time when water may be scarce. Fortunately, we can clean ourselves and our homes with unpurified water or even with grey water, helping reduce our overall water consumption.

We tend to think of water as a "one use" expendable commodity. But during a time of crisis, when any water can be scarce,

let alone potable water, we need to think differently. Since the water we have usually has to be pumped or hauled by hand, it suddenly becomes much more valuable. With that in mind, no water should be only used once. Rather, it should be used as many times as possible. Some examples of doing this are:

- Placing clothing in the tub, so that the water we use to shower with can also be used to clean out clothes

- Wash the floor with water that has been used for washing other things

- Flushing the toilet with water that has been used to wash the dishes

- Watering the vegetable garden with water that has been used for cleaning or bathing

Of course, if you don't have running water, you might not be able to flush the toilet either, as the water treatment plant may be out of order. In that case, the best thing to do, if you don't want to dig an outhouse, is to use a bucket toilet, lined with plastic bags. The bags can then be removed and tied shut, for disposal later when the sewage system is working again.

It will be impossible to shower in that time; or at least to shower like we're accustomed to. Without water coming out of the faucet, our tubs and showers will seem to be all but useless. But they can still be used for bathing.

I've spent a fair amount of time in third-world and developing countries, in places where there was no running water. To bathe, we'd take a five-gallon bucket and scoop a couple of gallons of water out of the cistern, taking that into the bathroom with us. A second plastic container, something about the size of a Cool Whip container was used to scoop the water out of that bucket and pour over ourselves to bathe. The hair was always first, as the water pouring over our bodies from washing our hair would wet our bodies. About ½ gallon was allocated to wetting down. Then we'd shampoo and wash our bodies. Bathing was finished up by using the rest of the water to rinse our hair and allowing that shampoo-laden water to rinse our bodies as well. It may not have been as satisfying as a nice, not shower, but it got us clean.

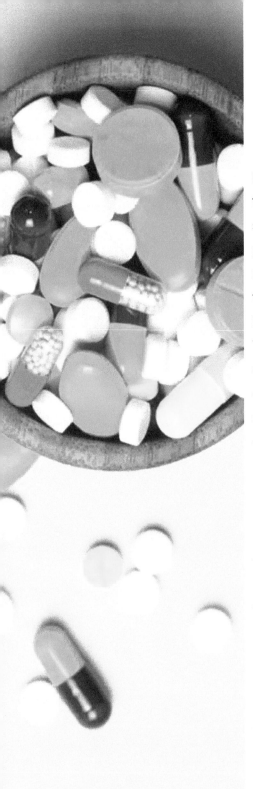

MEDICINES CHAPTER SIX: #6 PRIORITY

DEFENDING HOME & FAMILY

I started the last chapter by saying that there are things that can supersede our normal survival priorities, like injuries that require medical attention. The other area that falls into that same category is defending home and family. Two-legged predators tend to come out of the woodwork in times of crisis, especially when there are shortages. There's nothing like desperation to cause otherwise normal people to take desperate measures.

Before going any farther, let me say this; there are some people in the prepping and survival community who are gung-ho on going tactical, as if a survival situation will automatically cause a breakdown of society, to the point where we will have to fight for our lives. I think they've been watching too many movies. While that is a possibility, it's not very likely.

Civic-minded groups would probably step up to provide vigilante justice, long before society broke down to that point.

Nevertheless, there may be people who see a disaster and the disorder following one, as an opportunity to go looting. In addition, there may be people who become desperate enough to try and steal food and other necessities from whoever has it. We must be ready to defend ourselves from those people, just in case, while hoping that we never have to.

Please don't get me wrong here. I have a license to carry concealed and carry a gun every day. There have been two times when I was able to stop a crime in process by carrying. Fortunately, I didn't have to fire a shot in either case; my being armed was enough. But I'm smart enough to realize that no matter how good a shot I am and how well trained I am, there are others out there who are better. I don't want to get into an altercation with someone in a post-disaster world, because I don't want to take a chance on getting hit. A gunshot wound, without proper medical care, can be deadly. So, while I will use my guns to defend my family, I'll avoid using them if I can.

WHAT KIND OF GUN TO BUY

The first question that most people have is "What kind of gun should I buy?" That's both an easy and a hard question to answer. I can come up with some suggestions right off the top of my head; but those may not be the best guns for you. There's a lot of this that is opinion, regardless of what anyone says.

Basically, anyone in your family who is a shooter should have a pistol of some sort and a long gun (shotgun or rifle). Ideally, there should be an assortment of long guns, as they are all good for different things. The best guns for defense, aren't the best for hunting. The guns used for hunting big game, can't be used for small game or birds. Having an assortment

gives you more options; but it also means stocking more types of ammunition.

When I say "shooter" there, I'm referring to anyone in your family who is old enough and big enough to shoot a gun responsibly. If you're anything like me, you're going to want your family to hide, while you do a Rambo number to protect them. But I've got some bad news for you; you are no more Rambo than I am. So it would be best if you have some backup. Besides, if something happens to you, they'll need to be trained and armed to defend themselves.

Why a pistol and a long gun? One well-known firearms instructor put it this way, "You should carry a pistol, so that you have something to fight with, while you're making your way back to wherever you left your rifle." It may not be possible to have a rifle on you all the time, but you can carry a pistol all the time. A pistol is a defensive weapon only, allowing you to defend yourself at close range.

So, that brings us back to our basic question.

PISTOLS

Pistols fall into two basic categories: revolvers and semi-automatics. Those who are proponents of revolvers claim that they are simpler to repair. That's true; if you know how to repair them. The argument used in favor of semi-automatic pistols is that they are faster and easier to reload. I personally go with semi-automatics for that reason.

As for caliber, that depends on the individual. Nine-millimeter is the most common pistol caliber there is and is a pretty good choice for most people. The exception would be if the person's hands aren't strong enough to "rack the slide" loading a round into the chamber of the pistol. Some women have problems with this. In that case, they need a smaller caliber, like the .380 ACP or a revolver.

I carry a .45 ACP, semi-automatic pistol as my daily carry gun. My reasoning behind that is that if I ever have to deal with a criminal again, there's a good chance that they will either be high on drugs or high on adrenalin. In that case, the goal is to knock them down.

That's what the .45 ACP was developed for. But if I find myself in a survival situation, I'll set the .45 aside and carry my 9mm Glock.

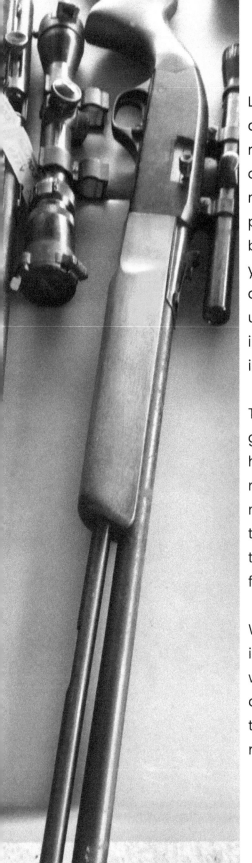

LONG GUNS

Long guns can include a number of different options, including hunting rifles and shotguns, machine guns and sniper rifles. The big risk with most of those is that they are too powerful. If you miss your target, the bullet will continue to travel through your wall, your neighbor's wall and anything else that gets in its way, until it finds something to lodge in. That "something" might be an innocent bystander.

The other problem with these long guns is maneuverability. Most hunting rifles and shotguns are rather long, making it difficult to maneuver them in the house. For that, you're better off with a shorter tactical shotgun or rifle. The choice for many is the AR-15.

While the round fired out of the AR-15 is still strong enough to go through walls, it is nowhere near as strong as the anti-gun crowd makes it out to be. Actually, as a hunting rifle, it's rather marginal.

But if your home is being attacked by a gang of people, that's probably the best gun to have.

The shotgun has been touted as the ideal home defense gun, especially when loaded with 00 Buckshot. It is a relatively close-range firearm that packs a lot of punch. Hitting someone with a load of buckshot is worse than shooting them with an AR-15. Just don't think in terms of the shotgun being a "point and shoot" weapon, like many people say. You're not going to get much spread out of your shot at the range you're going to be shooting to defend your home, so make sure you're pointed at a target, not just pointed in general.

PREPARING YOUR HOME

The average home isn't ready at all for an attack. The typical front door can be kicked open by a booted foot, even if it has a deadbolt. Windows are glass, so can be easily shattered. The conventional wisdom we're told about making our homes secure is good for protection from burglars, but those burglars don't want to attract attention. That's not the same as protecting from an attack.

DOORS

The most likely entry point for anyone trying to attack your home is through the front door. As I just mentioned, they can probably kick that open, even if you do have a deadbolt. The weak point isn't the deadbolt or even the door lock, it's the frame. That door frame is probably made of ¾" thick pine and the edge of the hole the deadbolt goes into is only about ½" from the edge. When the door is kicked, the deadbolt will break through that frame.

There's an easy solution to this, that's to install a security striker plate. There are two basic styles of these: one about a foot long and one that is three to four feet long. Go with the longer one. That will spread the force of the kick over a larger area, allowing it to dissipate and protecting the door frame.

When installing that security striker plate, be sure to use screws that are at least 3" long, allowing them to go through the door frame and into the structural studs behind it. While you're at it, replace the screws in the hinges with those long screws as well, eliminating another weak point.

WINDOWS

Windows are harder to secure, both because there are so many of them and because they are glass. The lower cost option is to install window security film. This is like tinting film except that it is clear and is considerably thicker. Once installed, it acts like the middle layer of a windshield, when the glass is broken, holding the glass in place. To get in, they have to break the window out, all the way around the perimeter. That takes time, allowing you to react.

The more expensive option is to install security bars over your windows. "Universal" bars area available from home improvement centers; but the best are the custom made ones that you can order from a welding shop. While that will cost more, they'll be made to fit your house.

The welding shop can also fabricate a gate to go over your home's sliding glass door, if you have one; making that secure as well.

LET'S TALK LEGALITIES

Before ending this chapter, I need to take a moment to talk about legalities. American law allows for the use of deadly force in self-defense and in the defense of others. Some states allow you the use of deadly force to protect property as well; but others require that you abandon your home, rather than standing your ground. Make sure that you know what the laws in your state say.

The possibility exists that there may be a total breakdown of law and order in a time of crisis. It's not highly likely, but the possibility exists. Even so, things won't stay that way and if you end up shooting someone, you can be sure that it will end up in court. It might take a while, but you'll be there. So, make sure that you're justified, before taking the shot.

Ok, so what makes you justified? The legal jargon says something like, "imminent threat of life and limb." That means that you or a family member will likely be killed or wounded if you don't take the shot.

It's a real threat, not an imagined one; and it can't be a threat that no longer exists, such as the bad guy turning and walking away.

The other big criteria that's used is what's known as the "reasonable man clause." In other words, were your actions the actions that a reasonable man, in the same circumstances, would have taken? That's a judgment call, so just make sure you fall on the conservative side of that question and you're sure that anyone else in the same circumstances would see the need to shoot.

OFF-GRID POWER

Amongst the many concerns we might have about surviving in the wake of a disaster is the lack of electric power. Let's face it, modern society is addicted to electricity, using it for almost everything we do. Yet there's a strong possibility that we won't have electric power available to us, even in the wake of a natural disaster, let alone a major event.

We've all seen it; all it takes is a windy storm or a winter blizzard to bring down power lines, leaving people without power. That's usually only for a few hours; but after Hurricane Katrina, some people were without power for six weeks or more. Worse than that, when Hurricane Maria hit Puerto Rico, it pretty much wiped out their electrical grid. There were people still trying to get by without power six months after that storm!

Fortunately, we don't have to depend on the grid for all of our electric power. While it is expensive to put in enough solar power to run everything in your home, it is possible to buy a few panels and be able to provide power for your most critical power needs.

Before getting into that, I need to mention that most solar power companies are less than honest; both in what they are selling and how they are installing it. Their advertising states that you can put solar panels on your home for no cost and lower your electric bills significantly. What they really try to do is sell you enough solar panels to meet your "average consumption," telling you that when you need more power, you can get it from the electric company and when you're producing too much, you can sell it to them. But what they don't tell you is that they won't buy electricity from you at the same rate they sell it to you for, so it will end up costing you a whole lot more than you expect.

The other thing they do wrong is that they install the panels flat on the southmost-facing side of your roof, not worrying about whether they are installing them at the optimal angle or not. They don't care if you get the most possible power out of your panels, they just want to make the sale.

One other thing I should mention, when you see solar panels for sale, they often are rated in watts; 100 watts is very typical. But that doesn't mean that the panels really put out 100 watts. That's a theoretical maximum potential that's never really reached. You'll always need more panels than you think.

Now with all that out of the way, let's talk about what you can do for off-grid power.

WHICH IS BETTER, SOLAR OR WIND?

For most of us, the only two practical means of producing power in our homes is either solar or wind power. Gasoline generators or whole house generators are useful for a short period of time (a few days at most), but they use so much fuel that you can't really use them for a prolonged period of time.

Solar is, by far, more popular than wind, which I think is more due to marketing and political pressure than any other reason. In reality, wind is more efficient and cost effective, in areas where there is enough wind to use it. That means having winds of 10 MPH or more, on a fairly consistent basis. If you don't have that, then wind won't work for you, just like if you don't have sun, solar panels won't work.

One problem with wind turbines is that they produce noise, which has led some municipalities to outlaw them. a vertical wind turbine, where the blades turn around a vertical axis, is much quieter than the typical horizontal wind turbine, where the blades turn around a horizontal axis (these are what we are accustomed to seeing). Vertical wind turbines also work at lower wind speeds and are non-directions. The problem is though, that they are more expensive.

Neither solar panels or wind turbines will produce power all the time; that's one of the big problems with using them to power our electric grid. But it's also a problem for you and I, when we want to use the for emergency power in our homes. There are two ways we can deal with this; use both, if we can and build a battery backup system.

THE BATTERY BACKUP SYSTEM

The core of any home electric power system is a battery backup system, not the solar panels or wind turbines connected to it. Those produce the power, but it is the battery backup which make that power usable; both by storing it and by converting it to the right voltage for use by your home.

- A battery backup system consists of three basic components:

- Solar charge controller (a 12-volt battery charger)

- Batteries (usually deep-cycle 12-volt lead-acid batteries)

- Voltage inverter (to boost the battery power up to 120 volts AC)

Many people spend a lot of money on a huge voltage inverter, but not enough on batteries. But in reality, the capacity of the system is based on how much battery storage there is.

That huge voltage inverter can't invert power that isn't there; so, you really shouldn't need one bigger than 1,000 watts.

On the other hand, you need as many 12-volt lead-acid batteries as you can afford. If you can, buy the deep-cycle ones, as they will last longer. Deep cycling of a battery means drawing off enough current to drop it below 50% charge, damaging the plates of the battery. Deep cycle batteries have thicker plates, helping them to survive this damage. But these batteries are also more expensive. So, you might want to buy a few deep-cycle batteries for the core of your system and see if you can get your hands on some used car batteries for the rest of the system storage.

One final point here. Because the voltage inverter needs to draw so much current out of the batteries, the wires leading into it are rather large. Make sure that any connections from the batteries to the voltage inverter uses large-gauge wire to avoid any risk of fire.

HOW MUCH POWER DO YOU NEED?

The first question we need to ask ourselves is just how much power we need. If you're planning on running your whole house off it, you're going to need to cover your roof with solar panels. Even that might not be enough. But we're talking survival here, not everyday living. For survival purposes, we need to figure out what our critical needs are. What are those?

- Refrigeration

- Some low-power lighting (LED)

- Perhaps one computer

- Well pump (if you have a well)

- Medical equipment (if medical support equipment is needed by any family member)

- Communications (charge phones)

That's not anywhere near as much power as we normally use, because I've left all the big power users off that list. What big power users? Heating and cooling, hot water, major appliances. Those are conveniences and not necessary for survival.

Even with our abbreviated list, figuring out just how much power you need is challenging. Both solar panels and wind turbines produce power at about 18 volts DC. That is used to charge 12 volts DC batteries. Then the power is drawn off the batteries and boosted up to 120 volts AC for use in the home. To do that, ten times as much power, as measured in amps or watts, needs to be drawn off the batteries.

Let me run through a quick example with you. The average refrigerator draws 3 to 5 amps of power at 120 volts AC. To get that, the voltage inverter needs to draw 50 amps of power out of the batteries, at 12 volts DC, in order to provide those 5 amps at 120 volts AC. If you only have one 100-amp hour battery in your battery backup system, you'll only be able to run that refrigerator for two hours before the battery is dead.

On the other side of the system, it's going to take several solar panels to provide enough power to charge just that one battery in one day. Solar panels only produce power 8 to 10 hours per day. So, they've got to be able to come up with the power needed during those hours. Wind turbines can work more hours and actually usually produce more power at night, so that can definitely help.

PREPARING FOR BUGGING OUT

For the most part, we're all better off bugging in, rather than bugging out. That's not to say that there is never a reason to bug out though. Back in 2017, the residents of Oroville, California had to bug out in a hurry, when it looked like the dam for Oroville reservoir was about to fail. Fortunately, the dam held and they were able to go back home. But the same can't be said for the residents of Paradise, California, who had to flee in 2018, when wildfires engulfed their town and burned it to the ground.

If we want to be prepared, we need to keep track of the pulse of what's going on in the world around us. I'm not talking about keeping track of politics; I'm talking about keeping track of potential natural disasters, terrorist threats, wars, chemical spills and other things that affect our ability to continue living as normal, in our homes.

Ideally, we need to be able to make a decision to bug out before there is any talk of a general evacuation. Should the entire city evacuate, you're just going to find yourself stuck in a 100-mile-long traffic jam. You want to beat that traffic jam, getting to your retreat before everyone else does.

There are times when we will get advance notice of a pending disaster that warrants bugging out. That's what happened to the people of Oroville, California. It also happened in 2005, when Hurricane Katrina hit the Gulf Coast and flooded New Orleans. Yet tens of thousands of residents didn't evacuate in the face of that disaster. That decision cost 1,836 of them their lives. On the other hand, there was no warning that Hurricane Harvey would stall over Houston, causing widespread flooding. It wasn't even sure that Harvey was going to hit Houston at all.

So, while our primary survival plan might be to bug in; it only makes sense to have a bug out plan as well. Preppers without a bug out plan might still bug out, but they're not going to be much better off than those who aren't preppers. After all, preparing is what sets us apart.

YOUR BUG OUT PLAN

Bug out plans don't have to be very complicated to be effective; but they have to be practical, as well as fairly complete. That means that the plan is something that you can do and have proven that you can do by going through a dry run.

WHERE ARE YOU GOING?

The first part of coming up with a bug out plan is finding a destination. Many preppers think of this as a "survival retreat" where they can escape society. That's a great dream and worth having, but few of us can afford to buy a cabin in the woods. All you really need is someplace you can go, which is far enough away from your home that it is unlikely to be affected by the disaster, while still close enough that you can get there, even if you have to get there on foot.

When the governor declared a statewide evacuation of Florida, before Hurricane Sally could arrive back in 2020, there were people having to drive as far as the northern border of Georgia and Alabama to find a motel with room available. That's because those people didn't have a bugout plan or anywhere else to go. Going to a hotel is fine, if you know that the hotel is going to hold a room for you; but if you don't have the kind of relationship with the hotel owner or manager, where you can count on that, you need something else.

For the most part, I like the idea of bugging out to a small rural town. I happen to live in one and I have developed relationships with some people in another one which is far enough away that they should not be affected by any natural disasters that I am. I can call the hotel there, asking them to hold a room for me, and I know they will. Not only that, but I know a couple of abandoned buildings in the town that I could camp out in and know enough people there, that they'll stand up for me.

About the only thing I could have which would be better than that, besides the cabin in the woods, is to have a friend or family member who lives out in the country, who I have an arrangement with, allowing me to use their home as my survival retreat. If their home isn't big enough, hopefully they'd have enough land that I could park a travel trailer there for shelter.

STASH A CACHE

In addition to having a location, you need to have a cache of gear and supplies stored there. With all the self-storage places available today, it's easy to find someplace that you can build that cache and it won't cost much money to rent it. Since you might not have time to do much packing, you're going to need to have those supplies available when you get there.

There are a lot of people living in the cities who think that rural communities will have lots of resources available, in the event of a disaster. That's not true. While they will probably be in better shape than any city center, they don't have a lot of resources sitting around. They've got what their residents need, and that's it. About the only exception to that would be harvest time, when grain silos might be full. But remember, those silos will be filled with only one type of food, probably a grain; definitely not enough for a complete diet. That's why you need a cache.

It's also a good idea to have some basic survival or camping equipment stored there as well, just in case you can't find a hotel room or abandoned building to use. If you camp anyway (which any prepper should – it's great training time), then keep your camping gear there. The only problem that will cause is that your camping trips will have to include a stop there to get your gear.

PLAN A ROUTE

The other thing that's needed to complete your bug out plan is a route to get from where you are to where you're going. You'll actually want to plan several routes, with crossovers to get from one to another, if needed. The major highways will be the first to fill up, so make sure that some of your routes are on secondary roads. Thirty miles an hour might not seem fast, but it's a whole lot faster than sitting still.

There is a possibility that you will be forced to abandon your vehicle and go it on foot, if you run out of gas or the roads get too clogged with stalled traffic. Many preppers buy 4-wheel-drive vehicles, with the idea of being able to go off-road to get to their survival retreat. But that doesn't mean you'll be able to do that. Someone owns that land you'd be crossing in your 4x4 and they might not want to allow you on their land. Should you be forced to abandon your vehicle and go on foot, about the only thing you'll be able to take with you are your bug out bags, one per family member. That will probably mean leaving some things locked up in your vehicle, which is why you want a good cache at your destination.

BUILDING BUG OUT BAGS FOR YOUR FAMILY

Considering that you will need to gather your family and go, as quickly as possible, in the event of a bug out, it only makes sense to be prepared, with everything you need packed and ready to go. That's what the bug out bag is all about; it can be considered to be a super survival kit, providing everything you need to have, as you make your way from your home to your survival retreat. If you have to leave everything behind, but your bug out bag, you'll be okay.

Many people talk in terms of "A" bug out bag, as if one bag is all they need. If you're single, that's true; but if you have a family, each member of the family should be carrying a bag. While not every bag needs to have all the survival gear your family will need; people will need clothing, a sleeping bag, rain poncho, water, water filter and their personal hygiene kit. As your kids grow, you can add other survival gear to that, like a knife, fire starting, flashlight, fishing gear, and communications gear. How much each family member carries depends on their age, level of training and physical strength.

Most preppers leave sleeping bags and tents out of their bug out bags, ostentatiously to save weight. But the backpacking community has had ultralight tents and sleeping bags for years, some of which are lighter than the alternatives that some preppers use. While I don't have any problem sleeping under the stars, with nothing but a rain poncho, I wouldn't expect my family to do the same.

It's usually best to build a bug out bag in a backpack, so that it will be easy to carry. Avoid a tactical backpack though, as they're too conspicuous, attracting the wrong type of attention. Rather, go with a standard backpacking style, which will have more room anyway.

Your pack shouldn't weight more than ¼ your body weight. That doesn't mean that if you're overweight, you get a bonus. In fact, if you're overweight, you might find that ¼ your body weight is too much to carry. Rather, go with ¼ of what your weight would be, if you were in shape. For a man, that means a load weight of about 45 pounds and for a woman about 35 pounds. Kids may only be able to carry 10 to 20 pounds. Let's look at the contents of a typical bug out bag. I'm going to break it down by categories, just to make it more understandable.

SHELTER

- Ultralight backpacking tent, big enough for the family or ultralight tarp to make shelter out of

- Rescue blankets

- Paracord

- Duct tape

- Ultralight sleeping bag

- Rain poncho

- 2 changes of rugged clothing, with extra socks & underwear

- Seasonally appropriate coat, hat and gloves

WATER

- Metal water bottles or camelback

- Bag-type water filter

- Straw-type water filter

- WAPI (for pasteurizing water)

FOOD

- 3 to 5 days of dehydrated food for the family (will be spread across everyone's packs)

- Aluminum or titanium backpacking cooking kit

- Collapsible cup or plastic cup

- Plastic plate or bowl

- Set of cutlery

- Salt and other spices

- Survival fishing kit

- Snare wire

FIRE

- 2 primary means of starting (stormproof lighter stormproof matches)

- 2 secondary means of starting (metal match, cigarette lighter)

- Tinder (dry material that will burn readily, like char-cloth)

- Fire accelerants

FIRST-AID & HYGIENE

- First-aid kit with sufficient supplies to take care of serious wounds, but not as big as the home first aid kit discussed earlier

- Toilet paper

- Personal hygiene kit

- Antibacterial hand cleaner

- Medical mask

- Insect repellent

- Soap

- Compressed towels

- Sewing kit (for repairs)

SELF-DEFENSE

This area is very personal and controversial. I would carry my sidearm and a rifle, along with a little extra ammunition, but each person has to decide what is best for them.

TOOLS

- Sheathe knife

- Saw (I've found a folding pruning saw to outperform any survival saw)

- Camp hatchet with hammer back end (for splitting wood and driving tent stakes)

- Folding shovel (I carry a Hori Hori instead)

- Multitool (optional)

- Machete (optional)

- Tactical light with extra batteries

One important factor here is to buy quality gear. Not only is the lightest backpacking gear the most expensive, it's also the best made.

GOING A STEP FURTHER

It's clear, looking at that list, that the bug out bag doesn't provide you with enough to survive for very long. For that reason, I recommend having some sort of push or pull cart that you can carry on the roof of your vehicle, for the purpose of carrying everything else along, if you have to abandon your vehicle. That will give you the ability to take along more food and water, a larger first-aid kit, more clothes and more tools; all of which will help your family to survive.

WHAT ABOUT A BUG OUT VEHICLE?

If you stick around the prepping community for long, you're going to hear a lot about bug out vehicles. The bug out vehicle is the vehicle that you're going to use, if you are forced to abandon your home. Some preppers get pretty wild with theirs, making some four-wheel-drive vehicle into the ultimate survival vehicle.

If you want to do that, that's fine; but it's not a requirement. Your bug out vehicle can be anything you own. Having a four-wheel-drive might be advantageous; but then, it might not help you at all. It all depends on your plan and your route, as well as what you run across along the way. But there are a few basic things that you need to take into consideration:

- **Size** – It has to be big enough for your family and everything you're going to take with you

- **Gas mileage** – Ideally, you want a vehicle that gets good gas mileage. You also want to take along extra fuel, because the gas stations will probably be sold out

- **General mechanical condition** – Probably the single most important thing in any bug out vehicle is its dependability. You want it to be in good mechanical shape and you want to keep it in good mechanical shape. A breakdown while bugging out will really ruin your whole day

- **Appearance** – Try to make it as inconspicuous as possible. If you've got a truck and there's survival or camping gear sticking out of the bed, it's going to attract the wrong type of attention, from people you'd rather not meet. You're better of with an inconspicuous mid-sized SUV, as there are lots of those on the road

FINAL THOUGHTS

Preparing to survive a disaster is more than a project, it's a way of life. People who get involved in prepping just think differently. Oh, it doesn't matter if you think differently when you start; by the time you've traveled this road for a while, you'll find that your thinking has changed. I've been doing this for over 40 years and I've found that readiness becomes part of life, something that you do, at times without conscious thought. Whether you're going to work or going on vacation, you'll make sure that you're ready for whatever comes.

This is a very worthwhile change to go through. If you've ever watched any westerns, those people lived their lives as if a disaster was about to befall them. They weren't the only ones either. Throughout history, people around the world have had to live that way. It's only in modern times that we've allowed ourselves to forget just how dangerous the world is and that tomorrow isn't guaranteed to us.

Preparing for whatever disaster might come your way is probably the most loving thing you can do for your family. Oh, they might not see it that way; but it is. It's making sure that they'll survive and there's nothing more loving or protective than that. They may never thank you and in fact you may not want them to; because if they thank you, it will be because your preparations saved their lives. Better that you prepare and never need it; but you can't count on that.

This journey is one that takes time, sacrifice and some hard work. Don't let that discourage you. Hundreds of thousands of others have trod this same road before you and many more will follow you. Those who have gone before will always be willing to lend a hand and share their expertise, if you can find them. in turn, you'll probably find that there are others you share with, who come along behind.

Preppers are a community within the wider community all around us. We make up people of every walk of life, every ethnicity and every socioeconomic stratum. But we all have one thing in common... the desire to protect our family from harm. That makes us all brothers and sisters in one regard. So... welcome to the family.

.

CPSIA information can be obtained
at www.ICGtesting.com
Printed in the USA
BVHW010858050822
643874BV00007B/73

9 781803 616544